A FIELD GUIDE TO YELLOWSTONE'S GEYSERS, HOT SPRINGS AND FUMAROLES

CARL SCHREIER

HOMESTEAD PUBLISHING
Moose, Wyoming

FOR BILL AND CHERYL

ACKNOWLEDGEMENTS

The author wishes to gratefully acknowledge the assistance and help provided by the National Park Service in the research and production of this book. In particular Linda Young provided invaluable assistance in locating documents housed in the Yellowstone Library. And Rick Hutchinson, Scott Bryan and Joe Halladay all provided critique and comments in the review of the manuscript.

PHOTO CREDITS

Scott Bryan (Valentine 19, Whirligig Geyser 21), Stephen Dobert (Echinus 23, Opal Terrace 13), Steven Fuller (Bison 4, Orange Spring Mound 15, Queen's Laundry 37), Jeffrey T. Hogan (Grand Geyser 65), National Park Service (Ledge Geyser 19, Vixen Geyser 23, Pink Cone Geyser 35, Narcissus Geyser 35, Beehive 71, Old Faithful 73, Lake Shore Geyser 89, Rustic Geyser 93), William J. Schreier (Steamboat Geyser 21, Steady Geyser 37, Opalescent Pool 53, Riverside Geyser 59, Grotto Geyser 61, Abyss Pool 87), Jennifer Whipple (Chocolate Pots 27, Surging Spring 89). All other photographs by the author, Carl Schreier.

Published by HOMESTEAD PUBLISHING
Post Office Box 193, Moose, Wyoming 83012

C O N T E N T S

GEYSER LIFE

Yellowstone is a country teeming with an estimated 10,000 thermal features. Of these only three percent are geysers. The rest are steaming pools, bubbling mud pots or warm seeps. Most geysers are small, and sputter and splash, barely reaching ten feet in height. There are only six grand geysers which erupt 100 feet or higher on a predictable daily basis. Old Faithful is one of these and erupts once approximately every sixty-five minutes.

Beneath the thermal basins lie the mechanisms which control these features. The most essential element is magma—underground molten rock. No one knows exactly how close to the surface this body of magma lies. Geologists believe the earth's crust is less than 40 miles thick here compared to 90 miles under most other land areas. There is a zone between the hot molten magma and the crust. It is a pliable layer of partially molten granitic rock close to its melting point. This zone heats water which has seeped down from the surface. The water filters through fissures, cracks, and porous rock and can eventually circulate to a depth of two miles. There it is heated by the molten granitic rocks to a temperature above its surface boiling point, but it does not boil because of the pressure in the underground network. As the superheated water works its way up through the subterranean chambers and conduits, pressure on it is relieved. The plumbing system traps superheated water before it reaches the surface and cools. Near the surface, when pressure is suddenly released, boiling explosions occur forming steam. The sudden expansion in volume then triggers a chain reaction leading to a geyser eruption.

Geysers vary in their length, frequency, and volume of eruption. Mineral cones have formed around some of their vents, like Old Faithful, Castle, Beehive, and Lone Star. Others are fountain geysers which contain a pool of water over their opening before they erupt. Great Fountain and Grand are examples.

The main natural plumbing system of a thermal feature is located near the surface, probably within 200 feet. A geyser must have a nearly vertical underground tube that connects with side chambers or porous rock, where water can accumulate. In some twisted networks water can cool substantially and ooze from the vent as a hot spring. In fumaroles water does not reach the surface. Only steam and gases come up its throat causing it to hiss and roar.

Travertine deposits.

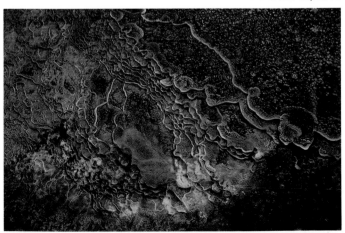

Ephydrid flies.

Geysers are a delicate balance between water and steam. A slight change in this balance can upset the schedule of eruptions. A pre-eruptive splash may upset this balance and trigger a major eruption or cause a delay. Man can also have this same effect. Coins, sticks, stones, handkerchiefs, and soap thrown into the thermal features upsets their balance and can cause a geyser to erupt prematurely, but more likely it causes it to clog, wither, and die.

Earthquakes also play a major role in upsetting the delicate balance of geysers. Near midnight on August 17, 1959 an earthquake, epicentered twelve miles north of West Yellowstone near Hebgen Lake, shook eight states. It measured 7.1 on the Richter scale, formed a twenty foot displacement, and carved a slab from a mountain side damming the Madison River. In Yellowstone thermal activity increased. Geysers began to erupt. some with new vigor. Dormant geysers awoke and hot pools surged with excess water. The earthquake caused some geysers to decrease in activity and it shut others off completely.

The thermal features of Yellowstone could not exist without the rock types found beneath the thermal basins. Hard minerals and rocks are needed to withstand intense heat and pressure. With the exception of Mammoth Hot Springs, most superheated geyser water passes through rhyolite and volcanic ash and tuff. These rocks consist mainly of silica, a hard mineral found in quartz and glass. When superheated water passes through these rocks it becomes laden with silica which is brought to the surface. Some of the silica deposits itself on the thermal features underground plumbing. The remainder is carried to the surface. During an eruption a geyser will splash the mineral-laden water around its vent. With ample time between eruptions the water will evporate, depositing the silica. Silica forms sinter, or geyserite, the rock formation which is built around these features. Sinter can form delicate scalloped edges on hot pools and elaborate cones on geysers.

Travertine is the deposit responsible for the famous Mammoth Terraces. The mineral—calcium carbonate—is carried to the surface like sinter, but it is dissolved in the heated water and precipitates into rinds or terraces as the water evaporates. Calcium carbonate is white or gray when dry, but various colors of algae add their brilliance, highlighting the delicate draperies.

In Yellowstone, hot springs, pools, and streams are the colors of the rainbow. Algae is mainly responsible for the brightly colored run-off channels. Different temperatures of water cause differences in plant communities and intensities of color. The run-off channel from a hot spring, for example, is white near its source. Only a few bacteria live in this 199°F water (boiling point at this elevation), and form long hairlike strands visible to the naked eye. As the water cools to 167°F, further down stream, the first blue-green algae begin to colonize. Pigments within the microorganisms are respon-

Predator spider.

sible for their colors. Chlorophyll produces grass-green, carotenoids form yellow, orange or red.

Large hot pools radiate with brilliant colors from deep blue to emerald green. Water reflects its blue color from the sky by absorbing the remainder of the color spectrum. A blue hot pool changes its moods from day to day with the sky and particulate matter in the water. When a pool is lined with yellow sulfur, the two colors produce hues of green.

Other plant and animal life thrive among the geyser basins. Small black ephydrid flies live on mats of algae. They swarm on the shallow run-off channels, feeding upon algae and bacteria, laying their bright orange eggs clusters on any small stick or rock projecting above the mat. During the winter they live a precarious life in a warm zone close to the water. If they stray away from this protective zone the cold air could freeze them in seconds. In the summer other perils take their toll. Predatory spiders, dragonflies, and killdeers pray upon and eat the small flies.

The warmth of the thermal basins stimulates the early germination of plant life. In the early spring when run-off is high and the ground is moist, yellow monkey flowers line the hot spring channels. By early summer purple fringed gentians cluster near the hot springs. Later in the summer when the basin soils dry, the yellow star-like blossoms of stonecrop appear on the nearly desert pavement.

Algae mats.

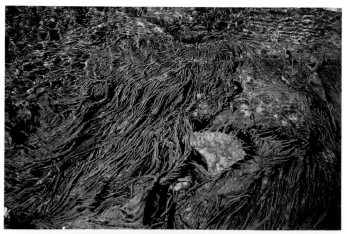

Fringed gentian.

A KEY TO THERMAL IDENTIFICATION

 A GEYSER

 A HOT SPRING

 A FUMAROLE OR MUD POT

MAMMOTH HOT SPRINGS TERRACES

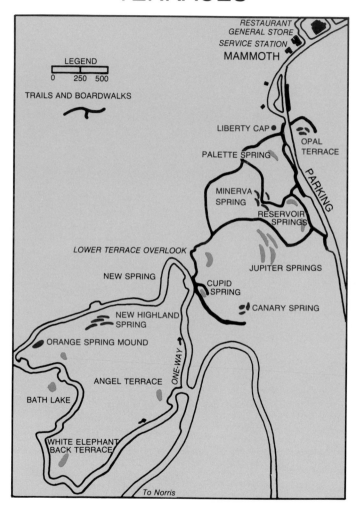

LEGEND

0   250   500

TRAILS AND BOARDWALKS

RESTAURANT
GENERAL STORE
SERVICE STATION
MAMMOTH

LIBERTY CAP

OPAL TERRACE

PALETTE SPRING

PARKING

MINERVA SPRING

RESERVOIR SPRINGS

LOWER TERRACE OVERLOOK

JUPITER SPRINGS

NEW SPRING

CUPID SPRING

CANARY SPRING

NEW HIGHLAND SPRING

ORANGE SPRING MOUND

ONE-WAY

ANGEL TERRACE

BATH LAKE

WHITE ELEPHANT BACK TERRACE

To Norris

The Mammoth Hot Spring Terraces have been a popular feature of Yellowstone since the early stagecoach routes up the Yellowstone River Valley. The Terraces were first described by the 1871 Hayden Survey, even though they were named and well known before 1871.

The step-like terraces are formed by heated water moving along the Norris-Mammoth Fault. The hot water carries dissolved calcium and bicarbonate to the surface of the terraces where pressure is released. Carbon dioxide then escapes as gas and the carbonate combines with calcium to precipitate as travertine.

The Mammoth Terraces are constantly changing shape and color. Springs which were active one to five years ago may be dry and lifeless now, but activity may resume again. Along with the change of thermal activity is a change in color. Fresh travertine is bright white in color and as it weathers it changes to gray. Bright-colored algae mats which were dependent upon a stable temperature and a flow of water also change as they die out creating a stark, bleak landscape.

LIBERTY CAP

Height 45 feet. It was named during the 1871 Hayden Expedition for its resemblance to the caps worn by colonial patriots in the Revolutionary War. The cone was formed from a steady flow of hot water emerging from a single source, depositing dense layers of travertine. The cone continued to grow as long as there was a source of water. Either the hot water spring found a more convenient undergdround channel to escape through or the orifice became sealed by travertine deposits. It is now an inactive spring and it is not known when Liberty Cap became extinct. The outer surface is weathered and now supports a plant community of lichens, grass and a small tree.

OPAL TERRACE   Temperature 160°F

When this feature was named by the 1871 Hayden Expedition it was a small spring with opal colors. It was dormant for a number of years until 1926 when it began to flow again. Since then it has been intermittently active. During the 1940's Opal was very active and rapidly deposited porous travertine, doubling its size. Nearly a foot of travertine was deposited a year. The terraces began encroaching on a tennis court and at first the deposits were rerouted. By 1947 the tennis court was removed and the terrace now covers the original site. Opal is now known for its pastel colors, but like most Mammoth features it constantly changes shape and color.

MINERVA SPRING AND TERRACE   Temperature 161°F

It is considered to be one of the most colorful and ornate terraces at Mammoth. Minerva has had periods of inactivity throughout its recorded history. But when it is active terraces are rapidly built of porous travertine. During the building of a single terrace, or terracette, travertine precipitates around the edge of a small pool, and can accumulate at an average rate of 8.5 inches a year. As the water cascades from terrace to terrace the water cools, allowing algae to grow. Blue-green algae, in colors of green, yellow, orange and red, line the terrace run-off channels.

ORANGE SPRING MOUND   Temperature 157°F

Mound dimensions 48 x 20 feet. It is named for the orange algae which streak the large travertine mound. The spring from this mound is cooler than other thermal features of Mammoth allowing orange-colored algae to dominate. The brilliant color changes from season to season depending on the flow rate and the amount of available sunlight. The mound appears to be a large cone-shaped hot spring, but it was actually formed along a fracture line of a fissure ridge. Several cones have formed along this line of fracture, including Tangerine Spring. The flow and deposition from this spring is low and the formation of this mound may be very old.

NEW HIGHLAND SPRING   Temperature 160°F

The Highland Terrace area was named by A.C. Peale, geologist for the 1872 Hayden Expedition. There are numerous springs and pools in the Highland Terrace area. Most are now intermittently active or inactive. New Highland Spring began its activity during the early 1950's. Before that time it was a grassy and wooded hillside. The Spring rapidly formed a massive deposit of porous travertine. The trees on the hillside were engulfed by travertine and now stand as skeletons. Like other thermal features at Mammoth, New Highland Spring changes from season to season depending on water flow and temperture.

CANARY SPRING AND TERRACE   Temperature 160°F

This spring is part of the Main Terrace, which includes Blue, Jupiter, Naiad and Main springs. All of the springs have had intermittent activity, but Canary has been the most regular spring in the group. The name Canary was in reference to the yellow filamentous algae growing along the edge of the spring, but Canary Spring is now known for its ultramarine-colored pool. The water flowing down the face of the terrace has created multi-colored bands of algae.

NORRIS
GEYSER
BASIN

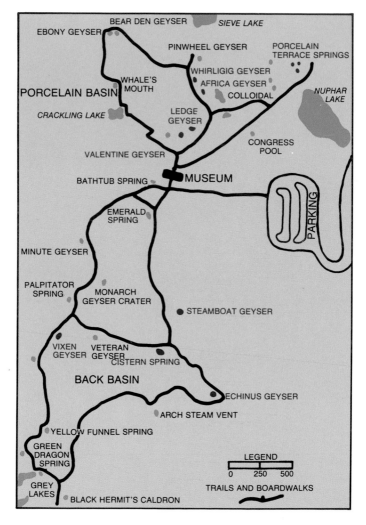

BEAR DEN GEYSER   *SIEVE LAKE*

EBONY GEYSER

PINWHEEL GEYSER   PORCELAIN
                       TERRACE SPRINGS

WHIRLIGIG GEYSER

WHALE'S   AFRICA GEYSER
MOUTH

PORCELAIN BASIN   COLLOIDAL   *NUPHAR
                                              LAKE*

CRACKLING LAKE   LEDGE
                        GEYSER

VALENTINE GEYSER   CONGRESS
                                  POOL

BATHTUB SPRING   ■ MUSEUM

                                              PARKING
EMERALD
SPRING

MINUTE GEYSER

PALPITATOR   MONARCH
SPRING   GEYSER CRATER

                        ● STEAMBOAT GEYSER

VIXEN   VETERAN
GEYSER   GEYSER
          CISTERN SPRING

BACK BASIN

                              ● ECHINUS GEYSER

               ● ARCH STEAM VENT

     ● YELLOW FUNNEL SPRING

GREEN
DRAGON   LEGEND
SPRING |_____|
                              0   250   500
GREY
LAKES   TRAILS AND BOARDWALKS
     BLACK HERMIT'S CALDRON

Norris Geyser Basin, named after an early Yellowstone Superintendent, is considered to be the hottest geyser basin in Yellowstone. The Carnegie Institute of Washington, D.C. made test wells in 1929 to determine subsurface temperatures. One test hole had to be abandoned at 265 feet when the temperature reached 401°F and the steam pressure threatened to destroy the drilling rig.

The stark, barren landscape of Porcelain Basin is the result of an acid environment. Because of this hostile condition plants and algae have difficulty in establishing themselves. Instead the basin is also colored by mineral oxides, in colors of pink, red, orange (iron oxides) and yellow (sulfur and iron sulfates).

The acidic water has also created changes in the formation of sinter deposited around vents. Silica may be deposited as tiny spines instead of thick, beaded deposits common in the more alkaline basins.

The largest geyser in the world is located here. Steamboat Geyser has long periods of dormancy, but when it does erupt it sends jets nearly 380 feet high in a spectacular display.

VALENTINE GEYSER   Temperature 197°F

Interval irregular-dormancy, Duration 60-90 minutes, Height 60-75 feet. Because this geyser érupted for the first time on February 14, 1907 from Alcove Spring it was renamed Valentine Geyser by C.W. Bronson. This geyser is very irregular, having seasons or years of dormancy. It erupts from a six-feet-high cone, located in a deep, wide alcove. The major activity of an eruption lasts only five to seven minutes jetting water up to 75 feet. This is followed by a steam phase lasting up to 90 minutes and gradually diminishing in height. It is a quiet eruption, unlike other Norris thermal features.

LEDGE GEYSER   Temperature 199°F

Interval rare-dormancy, Duration 20 minutes-2 hours, Height 75-125 feet. It was named in 1927 by J.E. Haynes for its position under a ledge of geyserite. It is the largest geyser in Porcelain Basin, but it is very irregular with periods of dormancy. When it is active it erupts from five vents. Before an eruption one of the small vents fills with water, splashing begins and progresses into a powerful burst of an eruption. The main jet arches at a 40° angle and jets out 125 feet. The other vents may also play up to 30 or 60 feet high. The main eruption lasts 20 minutes and slowly subsides after two hours. There is a rushing sound which accompanies each eruption, and the steam phase roars and rumbles.

PORCELAIN TERRACE SPRINGS   Temperature 203°F

This area of Porcelain Basin is stark and barren, nearly void of plant life. The uniqueness of this environment is created by acidic and low alkaline water. Sulfur is brought to the surface and oxidized to form sulfuric acid, creating a hostile environment for plant life. The springs have deposited a thin layer of procelain-like silica stained yellow and orange by sulfur and iron oxides. The crust is fragile and new springs are constantly forming and breaking through. Old vents from extinct springs are quickly sealed over by new deposits.

AFRICA GEYSER   Temperature 120°F

Interval 90 minutes, Duration minutes-constant, Height 45 feet. Africa Geyser first began erupting in February 1971. It was formerly a spring in the shape of the African continent. Africa Geyser is an example of the life and death of a geyser. When it first evolved eruptions were very regular, at nearly 90-minute intervals with plumes 45 feet high. Beginning in 1973 it was still active, discharging mostly a mixture of water and steam until Africa continuously declined and went into dormancy. Presently there is no indication, other than a small vent, that a geyser ever existed. However a new feature could become active nearby from a disturbance or by shifting thermal activity.

WHIRLIGIG GEYSER   Temperature 190°F

Interval minutes-hours, Duration 2-4 minutes, Height 10-15 feet. It was named by the Hague Party in 1904 for its whirling, puffing eruption. There are periods of dormancy during which a related geyser, called Little Whirligig Geyser, may become active. Whirligig Geyser begins an eruption cycle with a sudden filling of the crater progressing into an eruption. Most activity is from the central vent where an angled plume sprays at periodic bursts. Like many of Norris' geysers there is a roaring, hissing sound accompanying an eruption. There are subterranean connections between Constant, Little Whirligig and Whirligig geysers.

STEAMBOAT GEYSER   Temperature 198°F

Interval days-periodic dormancy, Duration minutes-hours, Height 100-380 feet. Originally named by the 1878 Hayden Expedition for its steamboat-like spouting. There have been name changes to Fissure and New Crater geyser, but Steamboat is the preferred name. Steamboat is considered the world's tallest geyser when it is active. Even though it has periods of dormancy, some lasting decades, it is a spectacular geyser when it does erupt. Eruptions are difficult to pedict. Before an eruption splashing begins, building into an eruption which may spout up to 380 feet. However if there is activity it is usually only splashing or minor displays which can reach up to 10-60 feet high. Because of the large amount of water needed for an eruption there may be subterranean connections with other thermal springs.

CISTERN SPRING   Temperature 194.1°F

Dimensions 27 x 41 feet, Depth 31 feet. This spring was transformed from a small gray pool to a colorful pool with terraces in 1966. The increased overflow engulfed trees and rapidly deposited a sinter terrace. Since then the terrace has been growing at a rate of 1.5 inches a year. When Steamboat Geyser has a major eruption the water in Cistern nearly empties. After an eruption it takes nearly one to three days to completely replenish. As a water reservoir for Steamboat, it is appropriately named. Brightly colored cyanobacteria distinguish the terraces of this spring.

ECHINUS GEYSER   Temperature 196°F

Interval 30-75 minutes, Duration 3-15 minutes, Height 50-100 feet. The sinter, spine-covered crater reminded early visitors of the spiny sea urchin. Echinus is from the Greek name for spiny. The crater is colored a light red-brown from iron oxides deposited with silica. It is the largest predictable geyser at Norris Geyser Basin. Before an eruption water usually fills the basin to within two-three feet of the rim and begins boiling. Churning and splashing then trigger an eruption throwing water and steam upward in a series of explosive bursts. After an eruption the basin drains with a whirlpool and gurgling sounds.

VIXEN GEYSER   Temperature 195°F

Interval minutes to hours, Duration seconds to 50 minutes, Height 5-30 feet. Superintendent P.W. Norris named this small geyser located along the trail of the Back Basin for its temperamental, spitfire disposition. It has a pink-colored vent stained by iron oxides deposited with silica. The geyser erupts from a round, cylindrical vent. Vixen has had two types of eruptions. One is minor activity every few seconds with occasional splashing and spouting up to 15 feet high. A major eruption will last up to an hour with water jetting to 30 feet, but these are rare and unpredictable. After an eruption the crater drains with gurgling sounds.

GIBBON
GEYSER
BASIN

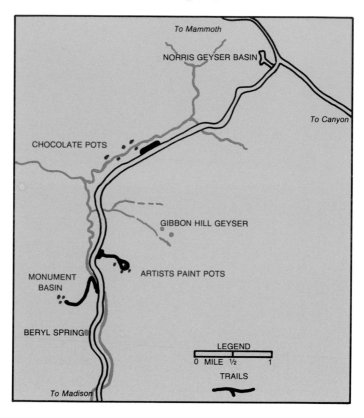

To Mammoth

NORRIS GEYSER BASIN

To Canyon

CHOCOLATE POTS

GIBBON HILL GEYSER

MONUMENT
BASIN

ARTISTS PAINT POTS

BERYL SPRING

LEGEND

| 0 | MILE | ½ | | 1 |

TRAILS

To Madison

The Gibbon Geyser Basin along the Gibbon River consists of the Chocolate Pots, Sylvan Springs, Artist Paint Pots, Geyser Creek, Gibbon Hill and Monument Basin. Each are small groups which are unique and different.

The Chocolate Pots are the most unusual group. They are a small collection of dark-brown cones colored by more than 50% iron oxide.

Sylvan Springs Group, located along the western edge of Gibbon Meadows, contains numerous small acidic hot springs, including Evening Primrose Spring. This spring was popular at the turn of the century. It was a deep crystalline spring similar to Morning Glory Pool. However, it has changed from an alkaline pool to an acidic pool. Sulfur covers the surface and a bacterium has changed the appearance of the pool.

Artist Paint Pots bubble and boil in colors of gray and pink. There are also several small constant geysers in the group.

Monument Geyser Basin is a unique group. Tree trunk-like cones mark this desolate basin.

CHOCOLATE POTS   Temperature 130°F

One of the most unusual formations in Yellowstone, the Chocolate Pots are located along the Gibbon River and the road between Elk Park and Gibbon Meadows. They are unique for their rich, dark-brown, chocolate color. The three to four-feet-high cones are streaked green by warm, water loving algae. Oxides are responsible for the dark-brown color. Iron, aluminum, nickel and manganese oxides compose nearly 60% of the pots, with silica composing an additional 17%.

ARTIST PAINT POTS   Temperature 185°F

The Artist Paint Pots are the most popular feature of the Gibbon Geyser Basin. They are an isolated group in the lodgepole forest at the end of a half mile hike. The group is named after the multicolored mud pots. Iron oxides have tinted the white mud pastel beige, pink and slate. The thickness of the mud varies from season to season. In the spring and fall the mud pots are "soupy," the thin mud bubbling and boiling. During the late summer the mud pots thicken and explode hot mud 10-15 feet high.

MONUMENT GEYSER   Temperature 194°F

Interval none, Duration steady, Height 1-3 feet. It was named by P.W. Norris in 1878 for its cylindrical cone. It is also called Thermos Bottle. The ten feet tall cone is thermos bottle in shape with a small diameter. It is a steady geyser, but it ejects very little water from the vent. A constant, low hissing sound is emitted. Because of its height and age, Monument Geyser is in the process of sealing its vent with internal deposits of sinter. Several nearby cones have already sealed their vents and have become extinct geysers.

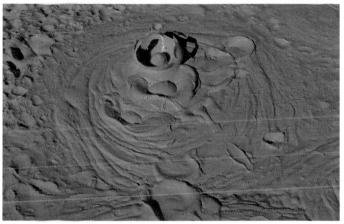

LOWER GEYSER BASIN

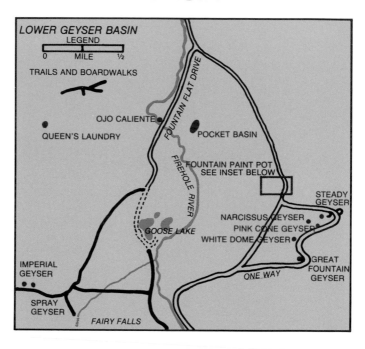

LOWER GEYSER BASIN
LEGEND
0 MILE ½

TRAILS AND BOARDWALKS

OJO CALIENTE
QUEEN'S LAUNDRY
FOUNTAIN FLAT DRIVE
POCKET BASIN
FOUNTAIN PAINT POT
SEE INSET BELOW
FIREHOLE RIVER
STEADY GEYSER
NARCISSUS GEYSER
PINK CONE GEYSER
GOOSE LAKE
WHITE DOME GEYSER
IMPERIAL GEYSER
GREAT FOUNTAIN GEYSER
ONE WAY
SPRAY GEYSER
FAIRY FALLS

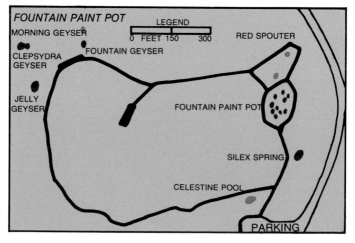

FOUNTAIN PAINT POT
LEGEND
0 FEET 150 300

MORNING GEYSER
RED SPOUTER
CLEPSYDRA GEYSER
FOUNTAIN GEYSER
JELLY GEYSER
FOUNTAIN PAINT POT
SILEX SPRING
CELESTINE POOL
PARKING

The Lower Geyser Basin encompasses nearly 12 square miles, with most of the thermal features widely scattered in small groups. Some of the groups include the Fountain Group, Firehole Lake Group, White Dome Group, Great Fountain - White Creek Group, and the Imperial Group.

There is a large variety of thermal features, including mud pots, geysers, pools, springs, and fumaroles. Great Fountain Geyser is one of the grand geysers in the Lower Geyser Basin. It erupts from a large, terraced platform with massive bursts exploding 200 feet high. White Dome Geyser does not have spectacular eruptive displays, but it does have one of the largest pink and white streaked cones in the Park.

The Fountain Group possesses a large cluster of multi-colored mud pots, and nearby in Pocket Basin is the largest collection of mud pots in Yellowstone. The Fountain Group also has several spectacular geysers. Fountain, Morning, Clepsydra and Jet geysers dominate the Group with periodic and colorful displays.

SILEX SPRING   Temperature 193°F

Dimensions 35.5 x 39.4 feet, Depth 27 feet. It is not known when or who named this colorful blue spring, but the name Silex may refer to the word silica; others believe it may refer to the Silex coffee percolator. The spring boils occasionaly and, periodically, large bubbles of gas rise to the surface. The 1959 earthquake caused it to erupt and increased the flow. The discharge is now 75 to 100 gallons per minute. There are underground connections to Celestine Pool, a similar nearby hot spring.

FOUNTAIN PAINT POT   Temperature 202.8°F

Dimensions 80 x 40 feet. Originally named Mammoth Paint Pots by turn-of-the-century tourists, it is now called Fountain Paint Pots. The mud is composed of clay and fine particles of silica broken down by acids and grinding action. The tinting of the mud in colors of pink and gray from iron oxides is derived from the original rock. The bubbling action is caused by escaping steam and gases - mainly carbon dioxide and hydrogen sulfide. In the spring and early summer the mud is thin and the pots boil. By late summer and fall there is less moisture and the mud is thicker, creating unusual shapes and formations.

FOUNTAIN GEYSER   Temperature 199.2°F

Interval 1-12 hours and occasional dormancy, Duration 30-60 minutes, Height 50-75 feet. Named by the 1871 Hayden Expedition, it is one of the most important geysers in the Lower Basin. It is located next to Morning Geyser, the largest geyser in the group, which usually has long periods of dormancy of one or more years. During Fountain's quiet phase the water is azure blue and tranquil. About an hour before an eruption a stream of bubbles rises to the sruface. The water begins to boil and churn resulting in an eruption. After an eruption the water level drops one and a half feet below the rim. There are subterranean connections with all geysers in the Fountain Group.

CLEPSYDRA GEYSER   Temperature 197.3°F

Interval seconds-30 minutes, Duration nearly constant, Height 10-40 feet. It was named in 1873 by Professor T.B. Comstock, a member of the Army Corps of Engineers Survey, for its regularity like the ancient Greek water clock. It is considered a nearly constant geyser, erupting from four vents. Two types of eruptions characterize Clepsydra. The constant splash-type eruptions from the highest vents send jets of water and steam 10-15 feet in all directions for about three minutes. The more powerful eruptions called "wild phase" activity send steady jets 20-40 feet from all four vents for three to six hours. The discharge is nearly 675 gallons per minute.

JELLY GEYSER   Temperature 196.7°F

Interval 15-90 minutes, Duration seconds-2 minutes, Height 1-10 feet. It is not known why Jelly received its name, but it was first described in 1873 by Professor Theodore Comstock of the Capt. Jones Party. It has one of the largest craters in the Fountain Group, measuring 16.5 x 30.6 feet. The edges are delicately scalloped with sinter. The indication of an eruption starts when the crater is full. The only warning before an eruption is a slight boiling progressing into splashing. The eruptions are small, discharging only 10 to 15 gallons per minute.

GREAT FOUNTAIN GEYSER   Temperature 202°F

Interval 8-12 hours, Duration 45-60 minutes, Height 75-150 feet. This is considered to be one of the grand geysers of Yellowstone. It has the distinction of having the first written description recorded by the 1869 Folsom-Cook Expedition. But it was not named until the 1872 Hayden Survey. The intricately terraced, sinter cone is 150 feet in diameter with a 14 x 20 foot crater. The eruptions begin about one hour after the crater fills and the first overflow spills onto the terraces. The overflow period is longer in spring and fall. A few minutes before the eruption water violently surges and boils initiating an eruption. The bursts may reach up to 200 feet, but average 100 feet. The hour-long eruption has several phases.

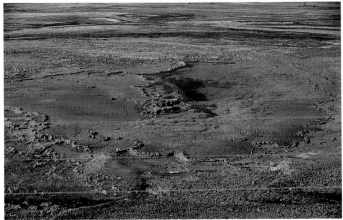

WHITE DOME GEYSER   Temperature 188°F

Interval 12-24 minutes, Duration 2 minutes, Height 10-30 feet.
Named by the 1871 Hayden Expedition, the name is
descriptive. The sinter cone, built upon an older hot
spring mound, is 20 feet high. It is an older cone built up
by spray. The orifice is now less than four inches in
diameter and it is believed that continued internal
deposition in the vent may seal it up. Moments after
splashing begins an eruption occurs. The eruption
begins with jets of water progressing into steam and
spray. The geyser is temperamental and irregular, but intervals between eruptions can occur from ten minutes to
one and a half hours.

PINK CONE GEYSER   Temperature 161°F

*Interval 6-15 hours and occasional dormancy, Duration 30
minutes-3 hours, Height 20-35 feet.* It was named by the
Hayden Survey for the beautiful shell-pink color of the
sinter in the cone. Manganese and iron oxides are
responsible for the dark color. The 18-inch-high cone is
located next to Firehole Lake road. During the construc-
tion of the road in the 1930's the geyser mound was cut
into, and the road now passes within 13 feet of the Pink
Cone. It has had periods of dormancy and its regularity
changes too. It erupts with a steady blast or column of
water with pauses and renewed vigor. There is no apparent underground connection with other thermal
features.

NARCISSUS GEYSER   Temperature 205°F

Interval 2-8 hours, Duration 5-10 minutes, Height 10-15 feet.
Narcissus was named during the 1880's by the Hague
Party. It was named after a Greek myth about a youth
who fell in love with his image in a pool. On his death the
gods changed his reflection into a flower called narcissus. This geyser is isolated behind a fringe of trees
north of Pink Cone Geyser. The six-foot-diameter crater
is lined with nodules of sinter and is a soft pink color.
There is a slow rise of water in the crater, and it begins to
overflow one hour before an eruption. Splashing triggers
jets of water 15 feet and sometimes 20 feet high. After an
eruption the crater drains and empties the bowl.

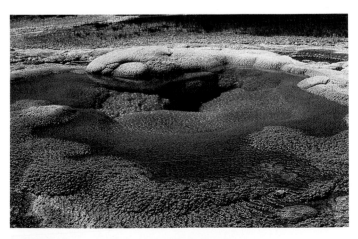

STEADY GEYSER   Temperature 199°F

Interval none, Duration constant, Height 2-15 feet. Named in 1871 by the Hayden Expedition for its constant action. The name was changed to Black Warrior Geyser in the 1920's but was changed back in the 1930's. It is considered to be the largest constantly erupting geyser in Yellowstone and the world. Steady is located on the edge of a small lake near Hot Lake. The dark gray-brown mound, colored by manganese oxide, is an irregular mass of built-up geyserite. Two vents and at times one vent may become dormant while the other continues to erupt. Steady has no known subterranean connections to other features in the Firehole Lake Group.

QUEEN'S LAUNDRY   Temperature 199°F

Dimensions 13 feet diameter, Depth 26 feet. The Queen's Laundry spring is a member of the Sentinel Meadows Group located on Sentinel Creek. It is a remote spring 1.5 miles west of the Fountain Flat Drive. There is no record of how it received its name, but it may have been named for the shape and size of its crater. The orange rim is raised eight inches forming a pie crust-like scalloped edge. The spring is constantly boiling with bright orange and yellow algae growing in the run-off channels.

OJO CALIENTE   Temperature 198.5-202°F

Dimensions 12 x 42 feet, Depth 32.5 feet. The Spanish name, Ojo Caliente, means "hot eye," for the shape of this hot spring. It is an isolated spring located near the bank of the Firehole River. The crater is surrounded by a heavy shelf of sinter, almost concrete-like in its appearance. On the northern end Ojo Caliente constantly boils, reaching 12-20 inches high. It has been known to erupt two to three feet high. The hot spring discharges approximately 100 gallons per minute.

POCKET BASIN MUD POTS   Temperature 188°F

Dimensions area size 1300 x 700 feet. Pocket Basin, on the eastern edge of a thermal crater, was formed by a hydrothermal explosion. This steam explosion resulted from overheated ground water that exploded into steam. Pocket Basin is in an isolated area along the Firehole River a quarter of a mile east of Ojo Caliente. This is the largest area of mud pots in the Park. Steam works its way through silica-bearing silt, producing bubbling mud pots in white to light-brownish-gray. This area is very fragile and delicate. Since there are no designated walkways this area is extremely dangerous.

IMPERIAL GEYSER   Temperature 200°F

Interval seconds-2 hours and occasional dormancy, Duration seconds-3 minutes, Height 6-80 feet. The geyser became active in 1927. By 1929 it was named by a popular contest among visiting newspaper men. The eruptions during that year were so violent that the plumbing system may have been damaged creating steam and pressure leakage. The geyser went into dormancy until 1966 when it began a near constant eruption. In 1985 Imperial again went into dormancy, but still continues to boil and churn. The 75 x 100 feet pool is also known for its clear, blue-colored water. The discharge has been estimated at 500 gallons per minute.

SPRAY GEYSER   Temperature 199°F

Interval 1-5 minutes, Duration 3-10 minutes, Height 10-25 feet. An old and popular small geyser, Spray has had regular eruptions since its early discovery. It has the same energy source as Imperial Geyser at the base of South Twin Butte. It is one of the few geysers that has a longer duration of an eruption than the inactive interval. When it erupts there are two main jets of water. The main column jets at a 70° angle and both jets spray with some of the water dissipating into steam. The vent and vicinity are covered in a lush mat of chocolate-brown colored algae.

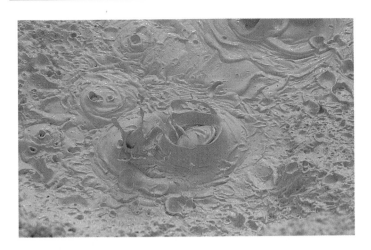

MIDWAY
GEYSER
BASIN

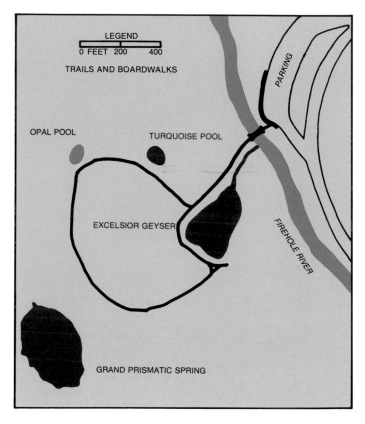

LEGEND

0 FEET 200   400

TRAILS AND BOARDWALKS

OPAL POOL

TURQUOISE POOL

PARKING

EXCELSIOR GEYSER

FIREHOLE RIVER

GRAND PRISMATIC SPRING

Midway Geyser Basin is a small collection of thermal features. It is part of the Lower Geyser Basin, but because of its location it is considered a separate group.

For its small size Midway possesses two of the largest hot springs in the world. Grand Prismatic Spring, which sits upon a mound surrounded with small step-like terraces, is nearly 370 feet in diameter. The other, Excelsior Geyser erupted nearly 300 feet high before the turn-of-the-century. It is now a dormant geyser and is considered a hot spring discharging more than 4050 gallons of water per minute. Other colorful springs include Turquoise and Indigo springs, known for their pale and dark blue colors.

Across the Firehole River from Excelsior and Grand Prismatic springs are a series of small isolated, pristine springs and mud pots along Rabbit Creek. Most of these features are unnamed, but they are colorful and unusual. There is no maintained trail through this area, and the ground is unstable.

EXCELSIOR GEYSER   Temperature 199°F

Dimensions 276 x 328 feet. It is considered to be the largest geyser in the world. However its last major eruption was during the 1880's, at which time there were numerous eruptions up to 300 feet. The violent eruptions of the 1880's may have caused damage to the siliceous sinter lining, allowing gas leakage and the loss of thermal energy. There were no observed eruptions until 1985 when it erupted for two days, however it only obtained a height of 20-80 feet. Since its active role in the 1880's Excelsior has been a productive thermal spring discharging 4050 gallons per minute. Numerous vents boil and churn the water within the crater, covering it in a dense layer of steam.

GRAND PRISMATIC SPRING   Temperature 147-188°F

Dimensions 250 x 380 feet. Grand Prismatic is considered to be the largest hot spring in Yellowstone. The spring sits upon a wide, spreading mound where water flows evenly on all sides forming a series of small stair-step terraces. It was named by the Hayden Expedition in 1872 because of its beautiful coloration. The brilliant colors begin with a deep blue center followed by pale blue. Green algae forms beyond the shallow edge. Outside the scalloped rim is a band of yellow which fades into orange. The outer border is then outlined in red. The spring is often shrouded in steam which reflects the brilliant colored algae. Grand Prismatic discharges an estimated 560 gallons per minute.

TURQUOISE SPRING   Temperature 142-160°F

Dimensions 100 x 110 feet. It was named in 1871 by the Hayden Expedition for its milky, white bottom and gemlike, blue-colored water. Suspended mineral particles in the water also adds an opalescent iridesence. Turquoise has no apparent overflow channel, instead water is lost through seepage. There is an underground connection with Excelsior Geyser. When Excelsior was active Turquoise lowered nearly ten feet and took nearly one year to recover. In June and July purple fringed gentians bloom on the barren ground surrounding this spring.

BISCUIT
GEYSER
BASIN

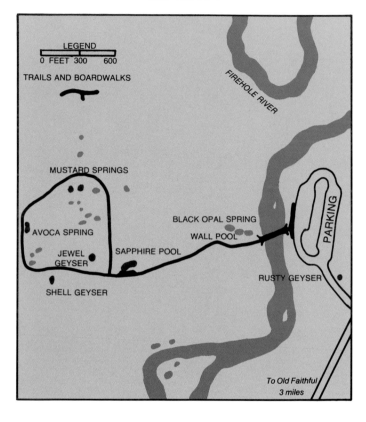

LEGEND

0 FEET 300 600

TRAILS AND BOARDWALKS

FIREHOLE RIVER

MUSTARD SPRINGS

AVOCA SPRING

JEWEL GEYSER

SHELL GEYSER

SAPPHIRE POOL

BLACK OPAL SPRING

WALL POOL

PARKING

RUSTY GEYSER

To Old Faithful
3 miles

Biscuit Basin is part of the Upper Geyser Basin. The biscuit-like sinter deposits which once lined the edge of Sapphire's crater prior to the 1959 earthquake were responsible for the name of this basin.

Biscuit Basin is a small collection of thermal features. Many, however, are small, gem-like pools and geysers, including Sapphire Pool, Black Opal Pool, Jewel Geyser, Silver Globe Spring, and Black Pearl Geyser.

The Basin is divided by the Firehole River and the highway. A smaller group, located east of the river, contains mainly hot springs. Cauliflower Geyser is the main feature of this group, and it is identified by the cauliflower or biscuit-like sinter masses surrounding the crater.

Sapphire Pool is considered the main feature in the group west of the river. The water is crystal clear and tinted the color of an Oriental blue sapphire. Other important features include Shell Geyser, which has a golden lined crater, and Jewel Geyser, known for the shiny, beaded sinter around its vent.

RUSTY GEYSER Temperature 202°F

Interval 2-3 minutes, Duration 20-45 seconds, Height 4-6 feet. This small geyser was named for its rusty, red-colored basin surrounding its sinter vent. Iron oxides are responsible for staining the sinter. This thermal feature was dormant prior to the 1959 earthquake. Since then, except from 1964-1967, it has been an active and frequent spouter. Its temperature is above the boiling point and this may be one reason why it is a steady geyser. The eruptions are spontaneous. Water splashes violently for the first ten seconds and then declines gradually in activity. Fumaroles are present around Rusty, but there is no known underground connection with any other thermal feature.

SAPPHIRE POOL Temperature 200-202°F

Dimensions 18 x 30 feet. Its name is derived from the blue, crystal-clear water with the qualities of an Oriental sapphire. After its discovery Sapphire was known as a placid hot pool. It was not until after the 1959 earthquake that major eruptions occurred. For several years later powerful eruptions reached 150 feet with two hour intervals. The crater doubled in size, the water was murky and the sinter ''biscuits'' around its edge were destroyed. By 1968 Sapphire ceased to function as a true geyser. It still boils violently and surges occasionally.

JEWEL GEYSER Temperature 199°F

Interval 5-10 minutes, Duration 60-90 seconds, Height 10-30 feet. Its name is descriptive of the pearl-like sinter beads formed around the vent. It was originally named Soda Geyser by the Hayden Expedition but the name was changed later by early visitors. The eruptions are frequent and regular. Before an eruption the vent suddenly begins to fill with water and churns to overflowing, triggering an eruption. A burst or jet of water projects 15-30 feet high and collapses, followed by a quiet pause. An eruption consists of a series of one to five separate bursts. Jewel does not appear to have underground connections to other thermal features but may have some connection with Sapphire Pool.

SHELL GEYSER   Temperature 200°F

Interval 1.5-several hours, Duration 20-90 seconds, Height 5-8 feet. The golden sinter lining of the crater resembles the shell of a bivalve, hence the name. Shell Geyser is very irregular and its interval between eruptions has changed from year to year. Before an eruption does occur water in the crater begins to rise and may overflow to boiling. Heavy churning then occurs setting off the first small, weak eruption. As the eruptions subside the water begins to lower and drain back into the crater. There are no known underground connections with other thermal features.

AVOCA SPRING   Temperature 199°F

Interval 1-18 minutes, Duration 10-30 seconds, Height 10-20 feet. Avoca was named by a member of the Hague Party during the late 1880's. The three-foot-diameter crater is located on a rise above the other thermal features at Biscuit Basin. It was not an active geyser until the 1959 earthquake. Since then it has been a frequent spouter, except for periodic changes in the interval and duration of eruptions. When an eruption occurs water jets in several directions from a filled crater. There is a pause between bursts, but the water continues to churn. The water drains from the crater as the eruptions subside. There may be subterranean connections with the Silver Globe group.

MUSTARD SPRINGS   Temperature 172-198°F

Interval 5-10 minutes, Duration 5 minutes, Height 4-6 feet. Two springs, East and West, make up this group. The springs are separated by 50 feet, they are four to five feet in diameter, and they resemble each other. They were named for the mustard-colored algae which line their craters. Although past earthquakes have changed their status several times from geysers to springs, both have erupted. West Mustard Spring was the most active between 1961-1983. A tremor in 1983 reversed this and now East Mustard Spring is a true geyser. The two springs have subterranean connections.

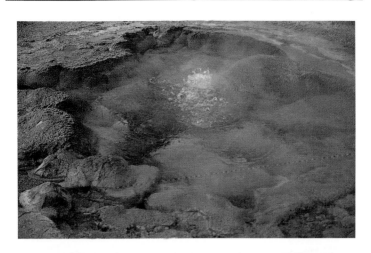

BLACK SAND
GEYSER
BASIN

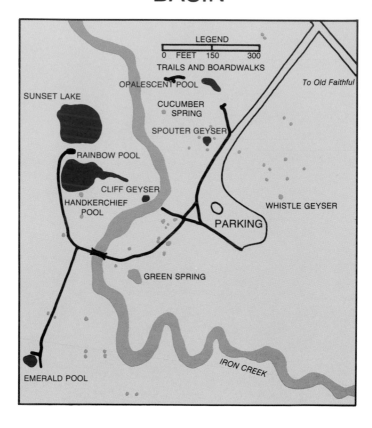

LEGEND

0   FEET   150   300

TRAILS AND BOARDWALKS

OPALESCENT POOL

To Old Faithful

SUNSET LAKE

CUCUMBER
SPRING

SPOUTER GEYSER

RAINBOW POOL

CLIFF GEYSER

HANDKERCHIEF
POOL

WHISTLE GEYSER

PARKING

GREEN SPRING

IRON CREEK

EMERALD POOL

Black Sand Basin, part of the Upper Geyser Basin, is a small collection of geysers, and hot springs. It was named for the black obsidian sand associated with this group.

There are a number of colorful pools and springs in this group. Emerald Pool is the most important and famous of these springs. It is a deep emerald green color with an outer ring of yellow and orange. Another colorful pool is Opalescent Pool. This recently formed pool has inundated a stand of lodgepole, creating a stand of white skeletons in a rainbow-colored pool.

An unusual geyser has formed on the bank of Iron Spring Creek. Cliff Geyser has formed a wall-like sinter ridge around its crater where it erupts 30 to 40 feet high.

The famous Handkerchief Pool was located here also. Turn-of-the-century tourists would drop their linen in this small spring to be whisked away, laundered and returned to the surface again. This spring has changed, but other just as interesting features have evolved since.

OPALESCENT POOL   Temperature 144°F

Dimensions 28 x 55 feet, Depth 6 feet. A colder pool than other thermal features at Black Sand Basin. There is evidence that earlier in its history this was a boiling spring. It was a small dry pool until the early 1950's when it began overflowing from the discharge of Spouter Geyser. The increased water flooded the surrounding area killing the lodgepole pine. Since then silica has precipitated up the trunks creating the white "bobby sock" trees. The silica, a non-crystalline compound, is slowly impregnating the wood and over time would eventually petrify it.

SPOUTER GEYSER   Temperature 199.9°F

Interval 1-2 hours, Duration 10-11 hours, Height 5-7 feet. Spouter Geyser was believed to be a continuous geyser. It erupts nearly constantly from a splashing, undulating, blue pool of water. The jets shoot through the pool reaching a height of five to seven feet. The crater is formed of sinter with scalloped edges and rosette beads. After an eruption the crater is drained. There is no known subsurface connection with any other spring in the basin. Overflow from Spouter flows into Opalescent Pool.

CLIFF GEYSER   Temperature 191.8°F

Interval irregular, Duration 30 minutes-3 hours, Height 40 feet. The geyser was named by A. C. Peale, geologist of the Hayden Expedition of 1872, for its cliff-like wall of geyserite formed along the edge of Iron Spring Creek. Before an eruption the crater will nearly fill with boiling water. An eruption then begins as jets of water explode through the pool 15 to 40 feet, accompanied with a great amount of steam. The first half hour is the height of the eruption, which gradually subsides, ending in two to three hours with an empty crater. The intervals of eruptions are irregular, lasting between a half hour to 18 hours. There may be weeks or even years of dormancy, but when it is active there are usually one or two eruptions a day.

EMERALD POOL   Temperature 154.6°F

Dimensions 27 x 38 feet, Depth 25 feet. Named for its emerald green color, it is one of the main attractions at Black Sand Basin. The color is the combination of lower temperatures which allow yellow algae to grow on the lining of the pool and the clear water which absorbs the color spectrum, except blue which is reflected. The two colors then produce hues of green. Objects which have been thrown into the pool have caused further decreases in temperature resulting in algae growth and a change of color. The edges are now orange and brown. If the temperature continues to decrease it will lose its emerald color.

RAINBOW POOL   Temperature 161°F

Dimensions 100 x 130 feet, Depth 27 feet. The edges of this pool are the color of the rainbow, hence the name. Algae and cyanobacteria are responsible for the varied colors. This pool has only erupted a few times in the past. During one eruption in 1948 it reached a height of 25 feet. The last known eruption was in 1973. There are underground connections with Green Spring and the famous Handkerchief Pool. Handkerchief Pool is located along the southern edge of Rainbow. It was a popular pool at the turn-of-the-century. By placing a handkerchief at one end of the pool convection currents would pull it down and a moment later it would reappear in another vent. It has not functioned since 1929 when it became plugged from human vandalism. It is now a small spouter and inaccessible because of algae mats.

SUNSET LAKE   Temperature 180°F

Dimensions 145 x 191 feet, Depth 23.5 feet. A shallow thermal pool with a soft sinter bottom. The edges are lined with yellow and orange algae. The pool discharges into Iron Spring Creek, and overflows into Rainbow Pool creating a large algae mat field between the two thermal features. Sunset Lake was not known to erupt until the 1959 earthquake triggered an eruption. The new surge of hot water killed the algae in the run-off channels. It has only erupted occasionally since 1959; during an eruption it surges three feet high but may reach eight to ten feet. There is no known underground connection to Rainbow Pool or other Black Sand Basin thermal features.

UPPER
GEYSER
BASIN

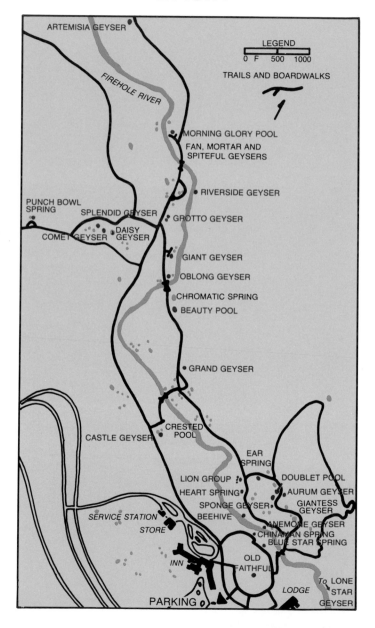

ARTEMISIA GEYSER

FIREHOLE RIVER

LEGEND

0 F 500 1000

TRAILS AND BOARDWALKS

MORNING GLORY POOL

FAN, MORTAR AND
SPITEFUL GEYSERS

RIVERSIDE GEYSER

PUNCH BOWL
SPRING

SPLENDID GEYSER

GROTTO GEYSER

COMET GEYSER

DAISY
GEYSER

GIANT GEYSER

OBLONG GEYSER

CHROMATIC SPRING

BEAUTY POOL

GRAND GEYSER

CRESTED
POOL

CASTLE GEYSER

EAR
SPRING

LION GROUP

DOUBLET POOL

HEART SPRING

AURUM GEYSER

SPONGE GEYSER

GIANTESS
GEYSER

SERVICE STATION

BEEHIVE

STORE

ANEMONE GEYSER

CHINAMAN SPRING
BLUE STAR SPRING

INN

OLD
FAITHFUL

LODGE

To LONE
STAR
GEYSER

PARKING

Many of the thermal features of the Upper Geyser Basin were named in 1870 by the Washburn Expedition. "We gave such names to those of the geysers which we saw in action as we think will best illustrate their peculiarities," stated N.P. Langford, a member of the Washburn Expedition. Those names included Old Faithful, named for its regular eruptions; Beehive Geyser, with its bee-hive shaped cone; and Riverside Geyser, named for its location on the Firehole River.

The Upper Geyser Basin, which is only approximately two square miles in area, contains the largest concentration and nearly 25% of the geysers in the world. A wide variety of thermal features exist here: spouting geysers, colorful hot springs, thundering fumaroles, and violent boiling springs.

Lone Star Geyser, which is actually in a separate group located four miles up the Firehole River from Old Faithful, has been included here.

ARTEMISIA GEYSER   Temperature 191-202°F

Interval 6-16 hours, Duration 10-30 minutes, Height 10-25 feet. It is believed this geyser was named by the 1904 Hague Party for the coloration of the sinter which looks like sagebrush. The scientific name of sagebrush is Artemisia. Artemisia Geyser has the largest crater ornamentation of any thermal feature in Yellowstone. The popcorn-like sinter has formed ridges and small pools 30 feet from the crater. Prior to an eruption there is a sudden rise of water in the crater and a heavy overflow. The water begins to boil and jets rise up to 20-25 feet. After an eruption water drops in the crater nearly two feet.

MORNING GLORY POOL   Temperature 171.6°F

Dimensions 23 x 26.6 feet, Depth 23 feet. A deep, funnel-shaped pool with a dark blue center. The resemblance to the corolla and color of a morning glory is responsible for its naming in the early 1880's. It has always been a popular thermal feature and a symbol of Yellowstone. The early stagecoach route and automobile road came within a few feet of this pool until 1971 when the road was rerouted. Early visitors removed the delicate scalloped border and contributed debris into the pool. In 1950 it was induced to erupt. Socks, bath towels, 76 handkerchiefs, $86.27 in pennies, $8.10 in other coins came up; in all, 112 different kinds of objects were thrown and removed from Morning Glory. The debris has contributed to the decline in temperature, causing algae to grow in the cooler water and forming the yellow and orange edge.

RIVERSIDE GEYSER   Temperature 201.2°F

Interval 7 hours, Duration 20 minutes, Height 75 feet. Riverside Geyser was officialy named in 1871 by the Hayden Expedition for its location. It is an isolated geyser with its own plumbing system, and it has one of the most regular eruptions of the major geysers in Yellowstone. About one to two hours before an eruption water begins to overflow and surge in the crater. Forty to 50 minutes before an eruption water may boil and splash from the crater. A heavy surge or splash then triggers an eruption. The column of water arches over the Firehole River at a 70° angle and at times spans the width of the River. The peak of the eruption is during the first five minutes and then begins to slowly subside followed by a steam phase.

GROTTO GEYSER   Temperature 201°F

Interval 1 hour-2 days, Duration varies, Height 20-30 feet. It was named by the 1870 Washburn Expedition for the "winding apertures penetrating the sinter." It is an unusual shaped formation nearly eight feet high. The club-shaped pillar and two adjoining arches are formed from fallen trees. The accumulation of sinter from eruptions and evaporation have changed their original shape into eery formations. The transfer of thermal energy from Giant Geyser to Grotto in 1955 has resulted in a productive feature. The eruptions consist of a series of powerful splashes, steam and the discharge of nearly 150 gallons per minute. Deep gurgling and splashing sounds are constantly emitted from the vent.

COMET GEYSER   Temperature 201.6°F

Interval steady (irregular), Duration steady, Height 5-15 feet. This geyser was originally named Spray by Dr. F. Hayden in 1878. Due to a confusion in the early description of the geysers within the Daisy Group their names became switched and the error was never corrected. Comet had the largest cone in the Group, suggesting it is a powerful geyser. However, water rarely splashes out of the crater, and rarely reaches 6 feet high. It has been a steady geyser with little change since its discovery. The only variance in its eruptive pattern can be attributed to the eruptions of Splendid and Daisy geysers and Brilliant Pool, indicating subterranean connections with others in the Group.

SPLENDID GEYSER   Temperature 199.4°F

Interval infrequent-dormancy, Duration 2-10 minutes, Height 120-200 feet. It was named by P.W. Norris in 1880 for its spectacular eruptions. Splendid was considered one of the major geysers before 1900, the year it became dormant. It was dormant until 1951 with occasional activity until 1959 when it became dormant again. In 1971 Splendid resumed its infrequent activity. An indication of a pending eruption is surging to 30 feet. The water rises from the crater like a fountain and begins erupting. There is an estimated discharge of 40,000 gallons during an eruption.

PUNCH BOWL SPRING   Temperature 199°F

Dimensions 12 feet diameter, Depth 30 feet. The name is descriptive of its punch bowl shape. The crater is a raised rim of sinter about 30 inches high. Water constantly boils and bubbles around the edge like a large, bubbling cauldron. During the turn of the century hot water was piped from Punch Bowl to a tent camp a quarter of a mile to the north. It is one of the few thermal features on which human tampering has had no disastrous effect. Ribbons of bright green and orange cyanobacteria line the run-off channels. There appears to be no underground connection with other springs.

GIANT GEYSER   Temperature 202.7°F

Interval 6-14 days-dormancy, Duration 1 hour, Height 150-250 feet. Named by the 1870 Washburn Expedition for its size and duration of an eruption, Giant Geyser is one of the major geysers of Yellowstone. It has rarely erupted since 1955. Prior to 1955 hydrothermal activity shifted cyclically from Grotto Geyser to Giant every four to five years, but since the 1959 earhtquake the energy has been vented through Grotto. Giant still possesses great thermal energy. It roars, splashes, steams and has one of the hottest vents in the Basin. The cone is also impressive; it is 12 feet high, broken on one side, and has an inside diameter of six feet.

OBLONG GEYSER   Temperature 196°F

Interval 4-13 hours, Duration 5-7 minutes, Height 20-40 feet. It was named in 1872 by the Hayden Expedition for the shape of its crater. The green-blue tinted pool and elaborate sinter formations around the crater are just as impressive as an eruption. Even though Oblong is not considered a major geyser, the eruption discharges a high volume of water. During the quiet interval there is a slow rise of water in the crater which can take one to three hours to fill. Eruptions are difficult to predict since there are occasional periods of turbulence and overflow. When it does erupt a fountain of water wells up setting off jets of water with splashing and steam.

BEAUTY POOL   Temperature 164-175°F

Dimensions 60 feet diameter, Depth 25 feet. This spring and Chromatic Pool are among the most colorful pools in the geyser basins. Their colors begin with a deep blue center radiating out to yellow, orange and red. There is a relationship between the two pools. When one pool began to overflow the water level in the other would drop. This periodic shifting in energy would be accompanied by a 10°F change in temperature. In recent years the water temperature has cooled allowing an increase in algae growth and a change in color.

GRAND GEYSER   Temperature 201°F

Interval 6-15 hours, Duration 9-16 minutes, Height 140-200 feet. The power and spectacle of a Grand Geyser eruption inspired the name by the 1871 Hayden Expedition. It is one of the few major geysers that has not changed considerably since its early discovery. The geyser erupts from a shallow basin filled with water. Two adjoining geysers, Turban and Vent, are separated by a thin narrow bridge. Grand's eruptive cycle is dependent upon the activity of these two geysers and West Triplet and Rift Geysers. Grand erupts during one of Turban's active periods. A slight ebb in Turban's eruption may signal an eruption of Grand with a sudden explosion and jetting of water.

CASTLE GEYSER   Temperature 200°F

Interval 9 hours, Duration 1 hour, Height 60-90 feet. It was named by the 1870 Langford-Doane Expedition for the similarity of the cone to the ruins of a feudal castle. The large sinter cone is nearly 12 feet high with a diameter of 20 feet at the top. Before the 1959 earthquake Castle was an irregular geyser with periods of dormancy. Since the earthquake it has a regular schedule with long eruptions. The water phase of an eruption lasts about 15 minutes, with a steam phase continuing for the remaining duration. Subterranean connections have been discovered between Castle and Crested Pool.

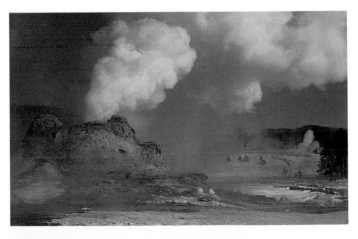

LION GROUP   Temperature 202°F

Interval 1-3 hours (irregular), Duration 2-4 minutes, Height 30-60 feet. Four geysers comprise the Lion Group - Lion, Lioness, Big and Little Cub geysers - and all are connected subterraneanly. The main geyser was named in 1881 by Superintendent Norris for its resemblance, when viewed from the south, to the body and maned head of a reclining lion. The largest cone and geyser is Lion which can erupt at intervals of one to three hours when it is active. A sudden rush of steam, like the roaring of a lion, precedes an eruption. There is a heavy discharge of water for a minute which declines into a steam phase for the remainder of the duration. The other features in the group also have dormant periods.

EAR SPRING   Temperature 202°F

Dimensions 4 x 6 feet, Depth 4 feet. A small but popular spring in the shape of a human ear. It was originally named Devil's Ear by turn-of-the-century tourists. Sinter forms the encrustation around its edge and along the overflow channel. It is a super-heated spring reaching temperatures of 205°F, and boils constantly. Surges have boiled up with heavy discharge after an eruption of Giantess Geyser and after the 1959 earthquake. There are subterranean connections with nearby springs.

AURUM GEYSER   Temperature 200°F

Interval 3-4 hours, Duration 60 seconds, Height 10-15 feet. A small geyser named for its soft pastel colors surrounding the vent. Iron oxides have been responsible for staining the sinter its peach and golden colors. Intricate, scalloped fromations have formed around the vent, creating unusual and symmetric patterns. In the past Aurum has had long periods of dormancy, but since 1985 it has been a regular, active geyser. Splashing begins an eruption which usually jets 10-15 feet high. There are no known underground connections with other springs.

DOUBLET POOL   Temperature 194.4°F

Dimensions 9 x 25 feet, Depth 8 feet. Doublet Pool is formed by two hot springs with identical sapphire-blue-colored water. A sinter ledge extends over the pool and two feet below this is another ledge, indicating that the water level was lower at an earlier time. It has been known to erupt, once during an eruption of a nearby geyser and after the 1959 earthquake. These eruptions were minor with the boiling activity only two feet high. The overflow is small, discharging only one to 20 gallons per minute.

SPONGE GEYSER   Temperature 199°F

Interval 1 minute, Duration seconds-1 minute, Height 1-2 feet. Sponge Geyser was named for its rounded, hole-ridden cone which gives it the appearance of a sponge. It is believed that Sponge is the successor to an older, more active geyser. The iron-stained sinter cone is now in the process of erosion. It is classified as one of the smallest geysers with most eruptions vayring between six to nine inches and rare upwellings reaching two feet. The eruptions occur at one minute intervals and consist of boiling. The water level drops and rises before another eruption.

HEART SPRING   Temperature 201°F

Dimensions 8 x 13 feet, Depth 16 feet. It was named because of the heart-like shape of the crater. This spring is typical of many of Yellowstone's thermal springs. It has been estimated that nearly 10,000 thermal features exist in Yellowstone and many are hot springs similar to Heart Spring in size and appearance. One feature which distinguishes each are the bright, colorful algae growing along the edge of run-off channels. One distinguishing feature is that Heart Spring has had temperature fluctuations from 150-202°F, allowing patterns of different colors of algae to grow.

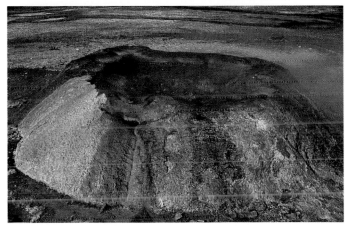

BEEHIVE GEYSER   Temperature 199°F

Interval 7 hours-days (dormancy), Duration 4-5 minutes, Height 150-200 feet. The 1870 Washburn Expedition named this beehive-shaped cone. The cone is three and a half feet high with a four foot diameter. It is considered one of the largest active geysers in the world, erupting to a height of 200 feet. However, it is difficult to predict an eruption. Since its discovery, Beehive has had a number of eruptive schedules, with intervals of eight to twelve hours to infrequent eruptions as long as three to ten days. The only indicators of an eruption are occasional splashing, then small surges which progress into an eruption. The ground rumbles as a narrow, straight fountain of water jets upward.

ANEMONE GEYSER   Temperature 200°F

Interval 5-20 minutes, Duration seconds-2 minutes, Height 3-6 feet. Anemone Geyser was named by turn-of-the-century tourists for the anemone flower. The geyser has two shallow basins nearly ten feet apart from which it erupts. The two vents, lined with sinter beads, act separately with minor eruptions occurring about every ten minutes to a height of three feet. Activity shifts from vent to vent, but they seldom erupt together. Anemone Geysers have no apparent subterranean connections with other springs.

BLUE STAR SPRING   Temperature 192°F

Dimensions 9 x 10 feet, Depth 6 feet. It received its name from the star-like sinter formation around the edge of the pool. Extensive ledges have formed three to four feet over the crater creating an illusion of a small spring. The ornate scalloped border of the ledge also extends along the overflow channel. This spring has had a history of vandalism. In 1946 the pool was cleaned and a pile of debris three feet in height by six feet in width was collected. There is no known subterranean connection with other thermal features. The spring discharges approximately four gallons per minute.

CHINAMAN SPRING   Temperature 200°F

Dimensions 28 x 34 inches, Depth 12.5 feet. A small spring located along the Firehole River. Chinaman has been known to erupt 20-30 feet high, but all known eruptions were man-induced. The first incident of a known eruption occurred in the 1880's when a Chinese laundryman pitched his tent over the spring and used the hot water as a clothes boiler. The clothes were suspended in the water by a wicker basket. The spring erupted for the first time and a column of water ejected the laundry and collapsed the tent.

OLD FAITHFUL   Temperature 199°F

Interval 30-120 minutes, Duration 1.5-5 minutes, Height 110-185 feet. Old Faithful was named in 1870 by the Washburn Expedition for its nearly regular schedule of eruptions. It is considered the grand old geyser of Yellowstone because of its frequent and predictable eruptions. The intervals between eruptions average between 65-75 minutes and the average duration of an eruption is about four minutes. To predict the next eruption the first continuous surge is timed until the final splashing. If the total eruption is less than four minutes the next eruption will occur in approximately 40-60 minutes. If the eruption is four minutes or longer the next interval will be 75-100 minutes.

LONE STAR GEYSER   Temperature 197°F

Interval 3 hours, Duration 30 minutes, Height 35-40 feet. Lone Star Geyser is an isolated geyser on the upper Firehole River. It was originally named Solitary by the 1872 Hayden Expedition. Its large, streaked sinter cone is 11.5 feet high. There is one large vent and several smaller apertures which constantly splash during the quiet phase. This splashing is responsible for the growth of the cone. An eruption is usually in two phases. The first phase may be a short eruption lasting three to five minutes with jets reaching 25 feet. After a period of 15-25 minutes the second phase begins with splashing, then continues with a forceful jet of water which progresses into a steam phase. The second phase lasts 30 minutes.

SHOSHONE GEYSER BASIN

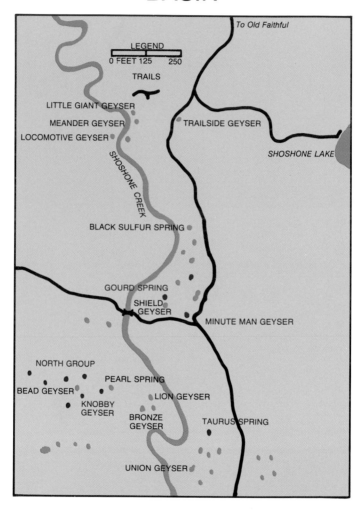

To Old Faithful

LEGEND

0 FEET 125 250

TRAILS

LITTLE GIANT GEYSER

MEANDER GEYSER

LOCOMOTIVE GEYSER

TRAILSIDE GEYSER

SHOSHONE LAKE

SHOSHONE CREEK

BLACK SULFUR SPRING

GOURD SPRING

SHIELD GEYSER

MINUTE MAN GEYSER

NORTH GROUP

PEARL SPRING

BEAD GEYSER

LION GEYSER

KNOBBY GEYSER

BRONZE GEYSER

TAURUS SPRING

UNION GEYSER

The Shoshone Geyser Basin is located   at the west end of Shoshone Lake. The lake and geyser basin were named and explored by Chief Geologist Frank Bradley and party, a group of the 1872 Hayden Expedition. However, Osborne Russell, an early explorer and trapper, may have been the first European to enter the basin in 1839.

This is truly a pristine geyser basin. Because of its remote location it is possible to enter this basin and find little evidence of man. The pools and geysers still retain their original formations of intricate sinter.

This small basin contains an estimated 110 thermal features, and many are geysers. Union Geyser is the largest geyser in the basin. It was active during the turn of the century, but it has had long periods of dormancy and has been dormant since the mid-1970's. The three small mounds, standing three feet tall, now show little activity. Minute Man Geyser is now the main attraction at Shoshone. It is a regular spouter with intervals of one to three minutes.

SOAP KETTLE   Temperature 197°F

Interval 9-21 minutes, Duration 1-3 minutes, Height 4-6 feet.
The large crater of this geyser is distinctive. Golden
sinter beads line the vent of the four-feet-high cone. It
has regular geyser activity, and an eruption can easily be
viewed. An eruption begins with water rising in the vent
and crater. As the water begins to overflow and boil an
eruption is triggered. Most of the activity is splashing
but there are bursts which reach six feet. After an eruption the crater drains and slowly refills with boiling water
for the next eruption.

GOURD SPRING   Temperature 196°F

*Interval minutes-hours (irregular), Duration 15-60 minutes,
Height 2-5 feet.* An elaborate, massive basin has been
built of sinter by the continuous splashing of water. The
crater is lined with white, beaded sinter, and the inside
rim is golden-colored. The crater measures ten feet long
by eight feet wide. The water is constantly boiling and it
does have occasional eruptions. The eruptions are minor
and usually consist of continuous splashing. The activity of Gourd is cyclic. Because corresponding changes
in water level are apparent, there may be a connection
between nearby Shield Geyser.

MINUTE MAN GEYSER   Temperature 180°F

*Interval 1-3 minutes, Duration 2-10 seconds, Height 10-40
feet.* Minute Man was named by Professor Frank Bradley,
Chief Geologist of the Hayden Expedition in 1872
because it erupted nearly every minute. It has a large
cone five feet high by 12 feet long built of gray sinter.
Before an eruption the vent and crater fill with water.
Boiling triggers a violent eruption as water is usually jet-
ted up to 10-20 feet high at first but declines in force until the water and steam are exhausted. A series of these
eruptions will occur for several hours and then the
geyser will enter a quiet period for another few hours until the cycle is repeated again.

TAURUS GEYSER Temperature 196°F

Dimensions 8.5 feet diameter, Depth 27 feet. Taurus Geyser is a deep blue pool. Orange-colored algae lines the edge and contrasts with the dark blue water. The spring is in a constant state of ebullition. It has erupted in the past during an eruption of nearby Union Geyser, the largest geyser in the basin which has long periods of dormancy. Taurus has erupted with bursts up to four feet high, but most activity is boiling and splashing.

KNOBBY GEYSER Temperature 192°F

Dimensions 11 x 13 feet, Depth 6 feet. A small spring geyser in the North Group. It is a white shallow pool, square in shape, with an intricate sinter border. The ornate rim is composed of white and gray rosette-like clusters. Knobby has cyclic eruptions depending on the activity of nearby Velvet Spring which has periods of long dormancy. The eruptive activity will last from one to three hours with occasional pauses varying in length. The duration and volume of each eruption has direct effect on the length of the pause. The eruptions can reach 10-25 feet high.

NORTH GROUP Temperature 189-199°F

This group has the largest collection of small springs in the basin. Some of the major thermal features are Glen Spring, Funnel Spring, Yellow Sponge, Knobby Geyser, Bead Geyser, Velvet Spring and Bronze Geyser. All are colorful, some are stained red and orange by iron oxides and blue-green algae in colors of green, yellow and brown. Intricate sinter borders have formed around many of the springs. All of the thermal features have high temperatures, and boil constantly.

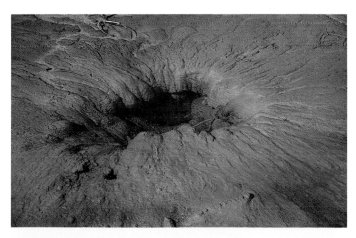

MUD
VOLCANO
AREA

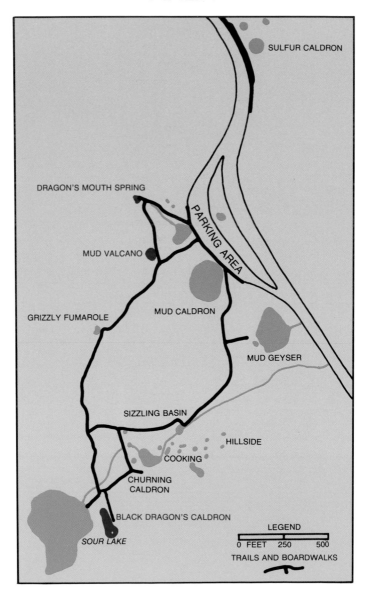

SULFUR CALDRON

DRAGON'S MOUTH SPRING

PARKING AREA

MUD VALCANO

GRIZZLY FUMAROLE

MUD CALDRON

MUD GEYSER

SIZZLING BASIN

HILLSIDE

COOKING

CHURNING
CALDRON

BLACK DRAGON'S CALDRON

SOUR LAKE

LEGEND

0 FEET 250 500

TRAILS AND BOARDWALKS

Mud Volcano was discovered during the early 1870's by the Washburn Expedition and the Hayden Survey. Both groups heard the sound "resembling the reports of distant artillery" for several miles before arriving at Mud Volcano. Mud Volcano at that time exploded with mud from its hillside alcove. Since then Mud Volcano has quieted but still remains a bubbling, seething spring.

The area is also known for Black Dragon's Caldron, Sour Lake, Mud Caldron, Dragon's Mouth Spring, and Sulfur Caldron. All are acidic springs. Iron sulfide is responsible for the dark-gray, black or brown-colored water, while hydrogen sulfide produces the "rotten egg" smell common to the Mud Volcano area.

Sulfur Caldron is one of the most unusual springs of the group. It has a high acidity of nearly pH 1.2, similar to citric acid, and the growth of a bacterium has produced a yellow-colored spring which contrasts to the other dark-gray or black, iron sulfide springs.

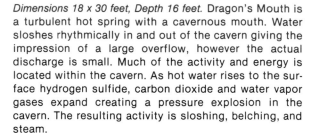

DRAGON'S MOUTH   Temperature 170.2°F

Dimensions 18 x 30 feet, Depth 16 feet. Dragon's Mouth is a turbulent hot spring with a cavernous mouth. Water sloshes rhythmically in and out of the cavern giving the impression of a large overflow, however the actual discharge is small. Much of the activity and energy is located within the cavern. As hot water rises to the surface hydrogen sulfide, carbon dioxide and water vapor gases expand creating a pressure explosion in the cavern. The resulting activity is sloshing, belching, and steam.

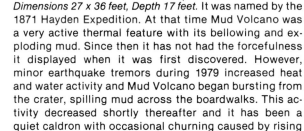

MUD VOLCANO   Temperature 184°F

Dimensions 27 x 36 feet, Depth 17 feet. It was named by the 1871 Hayden Expedition. At that time Mud Volcano was a very active thermal feature with its bellowing and exploding mud. Since then it has not had the forcefulness it displayed when it was first discovered. However, minor earthquake tremors during 1979 increased heat and water activity and Mud Volcano began bursting from the crater, spilling mud across the boardwalks. This activity decreased shortly thereafter and it has been a quiet caldron with occasional churning caused by rising gases.

BLACK DRAGON'S CALDRON   Temperature 191°F

Dimensions 80 x 200 feet, Depth 36 feet. This thermal feature did not exist prior to the winter of 1947-1948, and it was first discovered June 10, 1948. It is believed that thermal activity from Sour Lake shifted to form Black Dragon's Caldron. When it was first discovered a crater 43 x 68 feet existed at the northern end of the present pool. Since then eruptive activity has slowly moved 200 feet along a crack to the south. Hydrogen sulfide rising with the spring has reacted with oxygen to form sulfuric acid, creating a hostile environment for plant life. Iron sulfides are responsible for the black color of the caldron.

WEST THUMB
GEYSER
BASIN

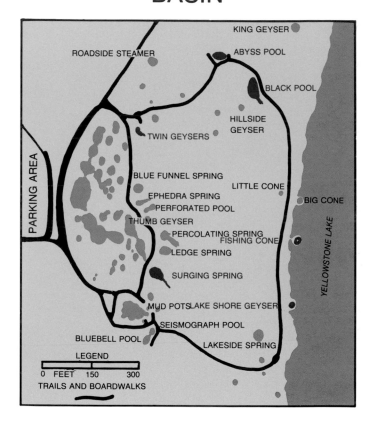

KING GEYSER

ROADSIDE STEAMER   ABYSS POOL

BLACK POOL

HILLSIDE
GEYSER

TWIN GEYSERS

BLUE FUNNEL SPRING

LITTLE CONE

EPHEDRA SPRING

BIG CONE

PERFORATED POOL

THUMB GEYSER

PERCOLATING SPRING
FISHING CONE

LEDGE SPRING

SURGING SPRING

PARKING AREA

YELLOWSTONE LAKE

MUD POTS LAKE SHORE GEYSER

SEISMOGRAPH POOL

BLUEBELL POOL

LAKESIDE SPRING

LEGEND

0   FEET   150   300

TRAILS AND BOARDWALKS

West Thumb Geyser Basin is one of the smallest geyser basins in Yellowstone, its location along the shore of Yellowstone Lake rank it as one of the most scenic. West Thumb derived its name from the thumb-like projection of Yellowstone Lake.

There is less geyser activity here than other basins. But West Thumb, for its size, has it all — hot springs, pools, mud pots, fumaroles and lake shore geysers.

Fishing Cone has been the most popular feature. Its unusual location along the lake shore and its symmetrical cone have been popularized by early stories of "boiled trout." Abyss Pool has also been popular for its deep water and colors.

The Thumb Paint Pots are constantly changing. In the 1920's and 30's they were very extensive and active. Now they are less active but, depending on moisture, they still build mud cones.

Since the mid-1970's West Thumb has decreased in thermal activity. Some temperatures have cooled in the basin allowing large colonies of algae and cyanobacteria to grow. As a result large mats of cyanobacteria flourish on the run-off channels and along the edges of pools where they did not exist before.

TWIN GEYSERS   Temperature 201°F

Interval irregular-dormancy, Duration 3-4 minutes, Height 60-120 feet. Twin Geysers are actually two vents together which have the nickname of Maggie and Jiggs, taken from early cartoon characters. The geysers have had periods of long dormancy. A 1934 violent eruption reached 120 feet and ejected water, mud and sticks. When Twin Geysers are active eruptions can occur every four to eight hours until it becomes dormant again. Even during dormant periods the geyser constantly bubbles and boils, discharging an even flow of water. Iron oxides have stained the area around the vent.

ABYSS POOL   Temperature 172°F

Dimensions 30 x 57 feet, Depth 53 feet. Abyss Pool is one of the most colorful and interesting pools in the West Thumb Geyser Basin. It was named for its abyss-like depth. The dark green-colored water is responsible for the illusion of a bottomless pool. Vandalism may have changed this pool's temperature. Coins and other debris thrown in have caused the vent to plug. The reduced water flow has also reduced the water temperature, allowing abundant algae growth along the edge and run-off channels. The extensive algae mats now support ephydrid flies, spiders and killdeers.

BLACK POOL   Temperature 132°F

Dimensions 40 x 75 feet, Depth 30 feet. Black Pool is one of the largest springs in the West Thumb Geyser Basin. The dark-colored water is the result of the natural blue of the water and the orange algae lining of the pool. The low temperature of the pool is responsible for the abundant growth of the orange-colored algae. The algae in combination with sinter deposits have created coral-like formations on the sides of the pool which are visible for only a few feet. The pH of Black Pool is slightly alkaline at 7.8.

FISHING CONE   Temperature 170.4°F

Interval dormant, Duration minutes-hours, Height 3 feet. Fishing Cone is a unique thermal feature to Yellowstone. It is situated on the shore of Yellowstone Lake and received its name for the fact that early explorers could cast their line into the lake and catch a fish. Without taking the fish off the hook they could parboil it in the vent of Fishing Cone. However the shoreline has changed since those times; Fishing Cone is usually inundated by high water during the early summer. It was known to erupt during the 1920's and 30's but the cold water of the lake has altered its eruptive behavior.

LAKE SHORE GEYSER   Temperature 198.6°F

Interval 30-60 minutes-dormancy, Duration 10 minutes, Height 20-30 feet. Lake Shore Geyser is very similar to Fishing Cone. It is also on the shore of Yellowstone Lake, and because of higher water levels the vent is usually covered by water. By August or September the water level is low enough for activity. However, Lake Shore Geyser has long periods of dormancy and geyser predictions are difficult. When it does erupt a column of water reaches 20-30 feet high and gradually decreases in force after ten minutes.

SURGING SPRING   Temperature 193°F

Dimensions 33 x 62 feet. Depth 28 feet. Surging Spring received its name from the occasional surges of water which overflow from the spring. The cyclic activity which occurs nearly every four to five minutes, begins with boiling activity a foot high. The water level of the spring rises and overflows for approximately two minutes. After a surge the water level drops four inches below the discharge channel. The overflow from Collapsing Pool may occasionally upset this cyclic balance. It is estimated that 162 square feet per minute is discharged during an overflow of Surging Spring.

HEART LAKE
GEYSER
BASIN

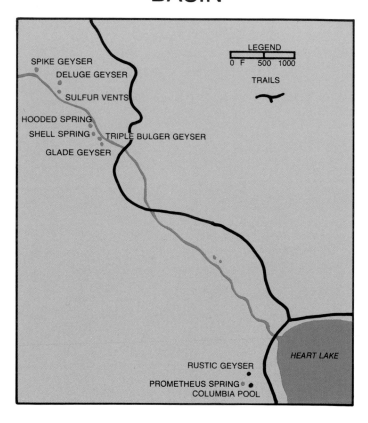

SPIKE GEYSER

DELUGE GEYSER

SULFUR VENTS

HOODED SPRING

SHELL SPRING ● TRIPLE BULGER GEYSER

GLADE GEYSER

LEGEND

0 F   500 1000

TRAILS

HEART LAKE

RUSTIC GEYSER

PROMETHEUS SPRING ●
COLUMBIA POOL

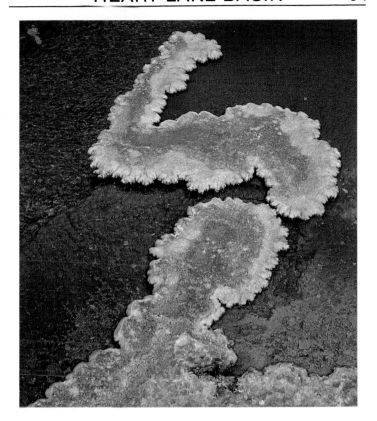

The Heart Lake Geyser Basin is a small isolated basin northwest of Heart Lake, located along Witch Creek at the base of Mount Sheridan and Heart Lake. The Basin was named by the Langford Expedition in 1870. A 5.5 mile hike through a dense lodgepole pine forest leads to a series of five groups of thermal features which make up the Basin.

Most of the features in these groups are fumaroles and hot springs associated with fissures. Because this area is secluded many of the thermal features have not been studied and named.

The main features are in the Rustic Group along Heart Lake. Rustic Geyser and Columbia Pool are located here. These features, like most Heart Lake thermal features, are in almost pristine condition. Elaborate sinter edges have formed around Columbia Pool. Logs which were believed to have been placed around the vent of Rustic Geyser by Indians or early explorers are still detectable under a layer of sinter.

The Upper Group has two important features, Spike and Deluge geysers. Spike has a two feet high cone and is beautifully beaded with sinter. Deluge is an irregular shaped basin with bluish-gray water. The edges are formed of rosette clusters of sinter.

RUSTIC GEYSER   Temperature 196°F

Interval 10-90 minutes and dormancy, Duration 1 minute, Height 20-45 feet. Rustic Geyser was named by the 1878 Hayden Expedition after they discovered logs placed around the geyser by either Indians or early explorers. It has long periods of dormancy, when it is active it is the major geyser of the Heart Lake Basin and erupts at regular intervals. Before an eruption water slowly rises near the rim and then suddenly surges to overflowing, bursting into an eruption of rapid spurts 30 feet high. As suddenly as it begins the eruption ends. Rustic also has unexplained periods of dormancy. Eruption intervals are influenced by high ground water in the spring and fall.

COLUMBIA POOL   Temperature 188.7°F

Dimensions 48 x 53 feet, Depth 25 feet. A beautiful azure blue pool named by the 1878 Hayden Expedition. Because of its remote location, Columbia Pool still retains much of its pristine condition. Large ledges project over the pool. The size of the pool and the stability of the edge is deceiving. There are no boardwalks through this area and much of the Heart Lake Geyser Basin has very unstable ground. Along the edge of Columbia Pool are white sinter deposits in the shape of rosettes. Orange and yellow algae surround the pool creating a beautiful display of color.

SULFUR VENTS   Temperature 110-180°F

On the slopes above Heart Lake and the Rustic Group, along Witch Creek, are the four remaining groups which comprise the Heart Lake Basin. In these groups are a number of sulfur vents. The small vents, ranging within a few inches in size, are fumaroles. They do not possess enough water in their craters to become hot springs, but below the surface water boils. What is emitted from the vents is steam. As the steam condenses in the cold air, steam-carried minerals are deposited on the outer edges of the vents. Bright yellow deposits of sulfur dot the barren hillsides and they sizzle and hiss.

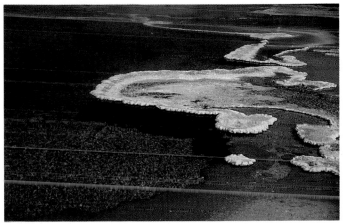

☐ A check box is provided next to each thermal feature so that this index can be used as a checklist.

Allen, E.T., and Arthur L. Day. 1935. *HOT SPRINGS OF THE YELLOWSTONE NATIONAL PARK.* Washington, D.C.: Carnegie Institution.

Bauer, Clyde Max. 1937. *THE STORY OF YELLOWSTONE GEYSERS.* Yellowstone National Park, WY: Haynes, Inc.

Brock, T.D., and M.L. Brock. 1971. *LIFE IN THE GEYSER BASINS.* Yellowstone National Park: Yellowstone Library and Museum Association.

Bryan, T. Scott. 1986. *THE GEYSERS OF YELLOWSTONE.* Boulder, Colorado: Colorado Associated University Press.

Marler, George D. 1973. *INVENTORY OF THERMAL FEATURES OF THE FIREHOLE RIVER GEYSER BASINS AND OTHER SELECTED AREAS OF YELLOWSTONE NATIONAL PARK.* Menlo Park, California: Geological Survey and National Park Service.

CONVERSION FACTORS

DISTANCE
1 inch = 2.54 centimeters
1 foot = .3047 meters
1 mile = 1.6092 kilometers

TEMPERATURE
Degrees Fahrenheit (°F) = Degrees Celsius
°F -32/1.8